FIRST IN THE HOUSE

Lorna A. Rainey

FIRST IN THE HOUSE

WOODBRIDGE
PUBLISHERS

276 5th Avenue Suite 704 #944

New York, NY 10001

Copyright © 2025 Lorna A. Rainey

ISBN (Paperback): 978-1-917526-69-2

ISBN (Hardback): 978-1-917526-70-8

ISBN (eBook): 978-1-917526-71-5

TABLE OF CONTENTS

DEDICATION

During the journey which is my Life, I have been blessed to cross paths with some extraordinary people. All of them were kind enough to share some part of themselves, whether they knew it or not. I have learned something from each one of them:

My mom, who was a never-failing fountain of Love, generosity, patience, tradition and encouragement.

My dad, whose Love of music and self-improvement, was the perfect counterpoint to my mom.

My maternal grandfather who could fix anything and would do it for complete strangers if I asked. Because of him, I can fix more things than most men.

My maternal grandmother who taught me how to fish, shell beans and find joy in sitting for hours on her back porch talking and listening to the far-away train whistles. Visiting her in Mississippi every Summer was how I learned about the invisible and sometimes very visible color lines of racism.

Uncle Junior was such a genius and first Black electronics chief in the U.S. Navy. Thank you for always pushing me to do better, be more and learn everything possible. In so many ways I am who I am because of you.

My brother…my confidant, hero, protector and Scrabble buddy who always popped up when I needed him.

My children for whom I try to set the best example. Our interactive Love continues to be the catalyst for all I do.

My son-in-law who is an exceptional partner and father.

My grandbabies.

Nieces, nephews, cousins.

All my relations, past and present.

My teachers from grade school through college.

My mentors in business who helped me learn to navigate "Swimming with Sharks."

Neighbors and friends.

My spiritual family…Medicine Priest, Chairman, Clan Mothers and committees.

And, of course, Aunt Olive who planted the seed, which continues to grow.

MISSION STATEMENT

This poem opens the book to set the tone for how I was inspired to make telling the story of the first Black Congressman one of the driving missions of my life. Olive Rainey was the only daughter of Joseph and Susan Rainey. I was destined to meet her so she could impress upon me the importance of her father's accomplishments and how the influence of a loving, dedicated elder can help the next generation recognize their mission. She always ended each storytelling with a kiss on the cheek or forehead and said, *"Lorna, you're going to be the one to tell everyone about his accomplishments."* Aunt Olive… that's just what I'm doing. ❤

"AUNT OLIVE AND ME"

From the young age of three I sat on her knee and heard the
story of old
About a man, Aunt Olive said was courageous, smart and
bold.
Year after year I heard about him in this very special way
And learned things I remember to this very day.

His name was Joseph and he was born enslaved
But once he gained freedom he became very brave
He did something no one like him had ever done before
I got so excited and couldn't wait to hear more!

So I got really comfy as she hugged me close
Her voice a soft whisper, it was just between us.
Aunt Olive smiled sweetly as she spoke of his glory
When you turn the pages then you'll learn the story.

Lorna A. Rainey © 2017-2025

THE BEGINNING

Joseph Hayne Rainey was born on June 21st, 1832, on a rice plantation[1] in Georgetown, South Carolina.

His parents, Edward and Gracia, were both enslaved, as was his older brother Edward Jr. That meant that Joseph was a slave too. According to the law, the children of enslaved people were slaves[2]. This is the type of cabin they lived in. Usually, there were only two small rooms. One was the main room for sitting, cooking and eating. The other room was a bedroom.

Photo: Exterior of a slave cabin in South Carolina.

Interior of a slave cabin from a South Carolina Plantation preserved intact at Hobcaw Barony Historical Research Center just outside Georgetown.

Imagine looking at your sweet baby and knowing they would have to work from sunrise to sunset in the fields when they were old enough! And continue to work until they were old men and women. There were no vacations or time off if you were sick. Even women who were pregnant worked every day until they give birth…then went back to work as soon as possible. It was a hard Life. As long as the slaves were healthy enough to work, they did. The only exception was if working might endanger their health. Slaves were valuable, so the masters[3] wanted them alive to help the owner make more money. However, the crops they produced were valuable too.

An authentic 1800s mortar and pestle used to separate the rice from the husks. The whole grains of rice were put into the bottom and pounded until the grains were free of their covering. This was a long and difficult process. If given this duty, the slaves worked on average 16 hours a day.

*Old slave threshing rice on a plantation, feeding the husks
to chickens.*

Rice field in South Carolina. Photo: Library of Congress.

The plantation had overseers[4] to make sure the slaves were working as hard as they could. It was all too much for Edward and his wife to accept. They would do whatever they could to get themselves and their children out of this lifelong sentence of forced involuntary labor.

As far as we can tell, Edward was the son of one of the owners of the Litchfield Plantation. The owners when Edward was born were the Tuckers.

Photo: Main entrance to Litchfield Plantation.

Photo: On Litchfield Plantation, trees, moss near the Abbey.

Most historians say cotton was the main crop on Southern plantations, and there was even a popular saying that *"cotton is king,"* and that's the crop we hear about the most. But in South Carolina, the main crop was rice! The rich soil and climate provided the perfect conditions for it to grow. Because of the huge quantities of rice grown, South Carolina was the richest state in the Union! However, to grow this much rice, the plantation owners needed lots of slaves to work the land, harvest the crops, get it ready for market and replant, starting the whole process over again.

Slaves would work every day, from dawn to dark, out in the fields. Imagine working in the blazing sun and heat all day! The only day they did not work was Sunday, and depending on the owner, maybe Thanksgiving and Christmas.

This was the hard Life that Edward wanted to save his two sons from. Although he was still enslaved, there were other jobs which some slaves could do with their master's permission.

Edward was allowed to learn the art of barbering. At first, he would only practice on other slaves. But after some time, the master let him cut his own hair as well as the hair of visitors to the plantation.

He developed a style which the master and his friends found very satisfactory. His skills were exceptional, and the men paid for his service. Although the majority of the money went to his master, by law, slaves who worked in jobs such as these had to be given a portion of their earnings. It was in this way, after about ten years, that Edward was able to buy freedom for his wife, his sons and himself.

They headed to Charleston to start a new Life.

DISCUSSION NOTES:

1 – A plantation was a large piece of land owned by a wealthy person. The plantation was used to grow a crop which generated money for the owner. Examples of cash crops are rice, cotton, corn and sugar cane. The plantations needed many people to work in the fields to make sure the crops were taken care of and picked at the right time.

2 – The enslaved people were people who were bought for a certain price and then belonged to the person who paid for them. They could no longer make any decisions for themselves. Their Lives and the Lives of any children belonged to their owner. Another name for these people was slave. Slavery is the name of the process by which people own other people. It is a system of forced/free labor.

3 – The masters are the same as the owners. They own the plantation and the slaves on it. They bought the slaves and legally claimed them as property.

4 – The overseers were the people the owner hired to make sure the slaves were working and doing what they were told. They always watched the slaves. To keep track of the slaves in every section of the plantation or other working area, they might be on horseback, walking or sitting nearby. They also measured what the slaves were producing each day during harvest time.

A NEW START

Once in Charleston, the family settled into a new Life. It was such a different experience from working on a plantation every day to the new opportunities and relative freedom of living in Charleston.

Edward right away was able to present his manumission papers[5] and get a job as a barber at the prestigious Mills House Hotel.

Mills House Hotel in 1863.

They had a salon there for the guests and Edward was paid handsomely for his skills as a gentleman's barber. This time, he didn't have to split his earnings with his master. He no longer had a master. He was a free man with a family to support!

Being a free man in the mid-1800s still had conditions. For example, authorities could stop you at any time and ask for your papers. There were slaves who had escaped from their plantations, but the authorities were always looking for them. They were called runaways and considered property. Slavecatchers[6] were paid a reward if they caught them and returned them to their masters. So, a freedman[7] always had to have the papers proving he was no longer anyone's property.

Manumission papers of a former slave named Caleb in Maryland.

Although it was against the law for any person of color to learn to read and write, enslaved or free, Edward Sr. was able to get a private tutor to come and teach the boys in secret. They had to be very careful about this. If anyone had found out, they would have been in big trouble.

DISCUSSION NOTES:

5 – The manumission papers were official documents registered with the local court. They were signed by a judge or magistrate as well as the owner to whom the former slave had belonged. They had to be carried and shown at any time requested.

6 – Slavecatchers were men who roamed the country looking for runaway slaves. Usually, on horseback, they traveled in pairs or groups to be able to tie up and capture the slaves who did not want to go back to the plantation. The masters harshly punished any runaways who were found and returned. The slavecatchers were paid for each slave they brought back.

7 – Freedman/Freedmen were formerly enslaved people (men, women and children) who had been released from slavery. Although they were no longer enslaved, they still were not considered first-class citizens and always had to be aware of any special rules or conditions which applied only to them. Another class of Freedmen were those born outside the country in places which had no slavery. They were free because of their nationality.

LIFE IN CHARLESTON

Edward Sr. knew what a good income he was making as a barber and decided to teach that skill to Joseph as well. Whenever he could, Edward taught Joseph the barbering trade…how to snap the towels, make a nice warm aromatic lather, sharpen the razor and make the customers feel pampered. Perhaps no other profession where the races interacted was more accepted than barbering. Just think about it: a Black man, enslaved or free, had a razor to the neck of his upscale white customers. Trust was developed between them. And there was usually free-flowing conversation. It was one of the most respected professions, and Black barbers were sought after.

Edward's job allowed him to provide a modest home for his family, which was quite different from the slave cabin Joseph had been born into.

They lived in relative peace and prosperity[8], although they still had to be careful to always have their papers[9] on them and have a white person who would vouch for their free status[10] if necessary.

Joseph took to the barbering trade right away and in a few years, he and his dad were working side-by-side in their own barber shop, Rainey's Hair Cutting Salon.

DISCUSSION NOTES:

8 – Prosperity is when you have enough money to live well.

9 – Papers means their manumission papers proving they were free citizens.

10 – Vouch for is when someone in authority or someone the authorities trust says you are telling the truth and you are who you say you are.

MARRIED, THEN SEPARATED!

In 1859, on a trip to Philadelphia, Joseph met and married a part French young woman named Susan. She was very beautiful, and they were very much in Love.

On the way back from Philadelphia, the young couple was stopped because Edward had crossed the state lines twice! Once when leaving South Carolina into Pennsylvania and then returning to South Carolina.

This was against the law! The authorities wanted all people of color to be accounted for in their own towns or cities.

Luckily, Joseph knew someone who came to vouch for him with the authorities. Once it was verified he was a free Black man of good standing and employed, they finally let them go.

The newlyweds decided to make their home in Charleston, where Joseph got a barbering job at the Mills House, the same hotel where he and his dad had worked previously. Things were going well for them, and then the Civil War[11] broke out! Even though he was a free man, the Confederates[12] went through the city, picking up all the able-bodied men including Black men to work for the Confederate cause. Since Black men were not allowed to own or handle guns, they were put to work doing hard labor on the fortifications[13] around Charleston.

He knew he had to escape! But how? The Confederate soldiers were always around...watching. However, one of Joseph's abolitionist[14] friends saw him and they hatched a dangerous escape plan.

His friends did help, and very soon, Joseph was on his way out of the country. But Susan could not go. It would have been even more dangerous for her to have come with them. If the Confederates had caught them, they would have all been killed! In a case like this, a person's skin color did not matter. The Confederates would have considered every one of them traitors.[15]

Taking great care not to be discovered, they had to use a less-traveled route, up through Nova Scotia on the East Coast of Canada and wait there for a ship his friends had arranged.

Joseph, with his guide to the next safe house on the Underground Railroad.

Although this was many miles away, it was a place where there were friends who were either abolitionists or other Black people whom they could trust. In 1785, 3000 Black Loyalists[16] had arrived in Nova Scotia. They lived in Halifax, Shelbourne and, most importantly, founded the largest free Black settlement in North America at Birchtown. Their descendants were always ready to help. He was in no danger there, but that was not the final destination.

After the long trip over land and by ship, he finally landed in Bermuda in 1862.

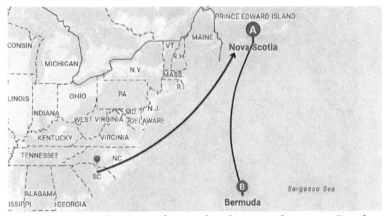

As shown in the map above, the distance between South Carolina and Nova Scotia to Bermuda.

He was safe!

The town of St. George's was the hub of activity and business in Bermuda, so it made sense he would settle there.

It was the center of shipping and commerce with throngs of people waiting for the ships coming in from England and Europe with more goods to buy or sell, work loading or unloading and experienced crew looking for the next job as a captain, steward, first mate, navigator[17] or as a cook on the voyage to the States. It was a good place to find work.

In St. George's, Joseph was able to set up a barber shop in the kitchen of a home called Tucker House.

Word spread about the new 'gentleman barber' from America, and in no time, he had a booming business.

Anytime he knew another ship from the States was arriving, he would go to the dock to see if his friends had also been able to help Susan get to Bermuda as they had promised.

One day…there she was!

DISCUSSION NOTES:

11 – A war between the Northern and Southern states over slavery and the rights of the states to determine what they were allowed to do.

12 – Confederates were the soldiers who fought on the side of those who wanted to be able to keep slaves. The Southern States were called the Confederacy.

13 – Fortifications are the high stone/brick walls around a place which stops the enemy from being able to come in.

14 – Abolitionists were people who believed slavery was wrong and worked to make it illegal. They helped slaves escape, wrote newspapers and gave speeches against it.

15 – Traitors are people who plot against their own country.

16 – Loyalists were people who pledged their loyalty to the King or Queen of England. They were also called the King's Loyal Americans.

17 – A navigator is the person who plots the course the ships must take to avoid shallow waters with hidden reefs, which could damage the bottom of the ship and cause it to sink. They also had to know how to plot a different course to avoid storms. They used hand-drawn maps and charts.

LIFE IN BERMUDA

Susan was an exceptional seamstress who made beautiful custom hats and dresses for women. She worked in the house too, building her clientele[18]. Between the two of them, they had a thriving business working from the kitchen of Tucker House, where they also lived. In order to help their businesses grow even more, Joseph and Susan took out ads in the local newspaper.

J. H. RAINEY,
BARBER,

HAVING Permanently Established himself in the Town of St. Georges—and thankful to his friends for past favors—begs leave to offer a continuance of his Professional Services to the Public, and hopes by strict attention to business to merit as heretofore, a liberal patronage.

Hair-Cutting, Shampooing Shaving,
&c., &c.,

Executed in Artistic Style.

His Saloon is situated in Tucker's Lane, or first cross street West of the Main Guard,

☞ Ladies, by intimation, may be waited on at their Residences.

May 11, 1865.

VIVAT REGINA.

Mrs. S. E. Rainey,
DRESS AND
CLOAK MAKER,
(Branch of Mme. Demorest's Emporium of Fashion No. 473, Broadway, N. Y.)

RESPECTFULLY announces to the Public that she has established herself

At the Town of St. George's,

where she is fully prepared to execute all orders in the above line

In the most Approved Manner and Latest Style.

Dress-making in all its branches.

Waists and Jackets cut and basted ; Waist Patterns cut to fit the form accurately.

Mrs. Rainey has for sale a few useful Articles for Ladies, and Children's wear.

IN ADDITION TO THE ABOVE

Ladies' Hair Dressed in all the latest Modes.
St. Georges, Nov. 27, 1865.—2

This is Tucker House, where Joseph and Susan lived and the kitchen area in which Joseph did his barbering.

The Bermudan people welcomed them warmly. The story of how they had escaped from the States during the Civil War made them even more admired. They developed a rapport with their customers, who introduced them to others, and the couple soon moved into the circles of Bermudan society.

Bermuda was a British colony[19], a part of the British Empire[20] and it remains a British Overseas Territory today. Their allegiance is to England and the crown[21]. Enslavement had been abolished[22] in Bermuda and the rest of the British Empire on August 1, 1834.

From reading Joseph's journal, we learn he was surprised that there was no more celebration on that day! He had expected parades, fireworks and jubilant people in the streets. But he observed that it was relatively quiet.

It was during his time in Bermuda that Joseph saw what was possible for POC[23] who were afforded equal opportunity, education and free will. He thought about all the enslaved people in bondage in America who had no access to any of those things.

Their clientele were sailors, merchants, dignitaries[24] and the upscale rich, representing all the types of people who lived in, passed through or were visiting St. George's. Their regular customers loaned them books so they could improve their language skills and read to them from local and United States newspapers. The couple were very interested in hearing the latest from the States. Joseph and Susan also studied the mannerisms[25] of the customers so they would be at ease in every situation.

They made themselves completely comfortable in Bermuda. Joseph became a member of a local political community organization and was very involved. It was called the Alexandrina Lodge. They wrote a letter of gratitude to President Abraham Lincoln for freeing the slaves, and 'Brother Joseph Rainey' was one of the signers.

Upon President Lincoln's assassination[26] in April 1865, they wrote a letter of condolence signed by over 150 members. It was signed and seconded by 'Brother Joseph H. Rainey.'

Now that the Civil War was over and the North had won, they heard that people of color were able to vote and Freedmen were even running for political office! Even though this sounded very appealing, the couple were happy with their Lives in Bermuda. However, when his father, Edward wrote and asked him to return, they did. In gratitude for everything the people of Bermuda had done for them during their stay, the Raineys took out an ad in **The Colonist** newspaper on September 25[th,] 1866 thanking them for their friendship and hospitality.

> *"Mr. and Mrs. J.H. Rainey take this method of expressing their thanks to the inhabitants of St. George's for the patronage bestowed upon them in their respective branches of business."*

They boarded a ship and returned to South Carolina. As a tribute to the place where the future first Black Congressman spent his days among them, the alley where Tucker House is located was renamed "Barber's Row," and there is a museum dedicated to him in the house.

DISCUSSION NOTES:

18 – Clientele are the customers for whom you provide a service or sell to.

19 – A colony is a country or area under the political control of another country and is considered part of the 'mother country' even though they may not be near each other. The rules and laws of the 'mother country' apply to them as well.

20 – British Empire are all the countries which were under the rule of England.

21 – Crown is another word for the King or Queen. The one who wears the crown. Also called the monarchy.

22 – Abolished means to become illegal, completely done away with and not allowed anymore.

23 – POC are any people of color. Their skin tones may be any shade of brown, red or yellow.

24 – Dignitaries are important people who are famous for their accomplishments in their field. They could be well-known in politics, business or social circles.

25 – Mannerisms are the ways people act which are common to that area, race or class.

26 – Assassination is the act of killing someone by a sudden or secret attack. A political person is usually the victim.

Here are the flags of Bermuda and the United States as they appeared in 1866. Bermuda has the flag of Britain, the Union Jack, and also depicts three ships in dry dock.[27] The American flag of 1866 had only 36 stars to symbolize the 36 states which made up the United States at that time. However, the red and white stripe layout was and still is 13. Throughout the late 1800s, more States would join and that continued until 1959 when both Alaska and Hawaii became States. Alaska joined in January, and Hawaii joined in August. Even though the United States has several protectorates,[28] such as Puerto Rico and the U.S. Virgin Islands, no more have been approved to officially join. So, the current number stands at 50, and the flag has 50 stars, one for each state.

DISCUSSION NOTES:

27 – A dry dock is a place where ships are built and/or taken out of the water to be repaired.

28 – Protectorates are territories which are controlled and protected by another country, mostly for defense and foreign affairs. They have some degree of self-rule.

GOODBYE BERMUDA – HELLO CHARLESTON!

Joseph and Susan were in a position that most other Freedmen were not. They came back to South Carolina with money from their successful businesses in Bermuda. And they were well-educated, having been mentored[29] by the many people they met in St. George's and the capitol, Hamilton. Although Black people in America had been granted their freedom by the Emancipation Proclamation, there was a lot of resentment and discrimination. They still did not have full rights to determine their own future.

After seeing what was possible for the people of Bermuda, Joseph decided that he wanted the Freedmen in the United States to have those same opportunities. The only way to help achieve that was to become involved in politics. From his time in Bermuda, he had also learned to communicate well with all classes of people, to be at ease with everyone, and he had read all types of books. He had practiced his penmanship until his handwriting was beautiful and flowing. Joseph was well-prepared to become a leader in State politics and a voice for the people who needed it most.

At the time, the Republican Party was building up its membership by welcoming all people to join. They had a platform[30] which was good for everyone. This was his chance! Joseph joined the Republican Party in South Carolina and soon became one of its most prominent[31] members.

He worked to help the Party enroll more members, and of course, many of them were people of color. As Joseph continued to help the Party grow, he also gained more influence and popularity. He was known as a tireless organizer, and the Republican Party became a beacon of hope for people whose voices had never been heard before.

After having lived in Charleston for about one year, he and Susan moved to Georgetown in 1867. He continued working, but his interest in politics grew, and soon, he was one of the executive committee members for the Republican Party of South Carolina. In early 1868, he was one of three Georgetown delegates to the South Carolina Republican Convention.[32]

At this Convention, many important issues were decided. Because the South had waged war against the Northern States (which represented the government of the United States), some delegates did not want former Confederates to be elected to any political office and wanted them to pay to cover some of the debts caused by the Civil War. Some wanted the landowners' property to be seized and auctioned off to pay their debts. Mr. Rainey spoke out against this since many people who still worked and lived on the land would then have no jobs nor anywhere to live. The economy in the South had been mostly wiped out during the war and many Northern whites had relocated to the South to pursue business opportunities. They joined the diverse people there to build a strong Republican coalition[33], which provided jobs and new opportunities. They became allies in rebuilding the infrastructure[34] destroyed during the war.

DISCUSSION NOTES:

29 – Mentored means to focus on a particular person to teach them what you know in your field.

30 – Platform is the course of action in which a political party, candidate or business describes their policies.

31 – Prominent: well-known or important.

32 – A convention is a large gathering of people to officially discuss or agree on political decisions which become binding.

33 – A coalition is a group of people working together for the same cause, a partnership.

34 – Infrastructure is a network of physical structures and facilities needed for the operation of a business, society or nation.

THE PATH TO POLITICAL POWER

During South Carolina's State convention, Mr. Rainey made a name for himself by introducing resolutions[35], which solved two issues of concern in the State. One was the issue of land distribution. Some freedmen were waiting for the government to give them a parcel[36] of land, but that would have come from the seizing of land from Southern landowners. He felt that the only way to own land was to purchase it. And he wanted to be sure that new schools could be built to offer education to everyone. He suggested a poll tax of $1 per year per person of voting age to fund this effort.

He was outspoken with his reasons and made a name for himself.

After the convention, he was elected to the South Carolina State Senate and served as the Chairman of the Finance Committee.

But he was not alone. There were many other people of color in the State legislature. African-Americans were a majority in the State Houses from 1868 through 1874.

RADICAL MEMBERS
OF THE So. Co. LEGISLATURE.

A photo of the first South Carolina legislature after the Civil War taken in 1868.

State Senator Rainey appears in the lower right corner.

With these progressive Republicans in control of the Governor's mansion, legislature, and Black officeholders in the State, big changes were about to take place. This change was called Reconstruction[37]...and it wasn't only in South Carolina. It was a wave which swept over the entire nation once the 14th Amendment, giving voting rights to every citizen, was ratified[38] in 1868.

That same year, he was elected to the South Carolina State Senate, where he served for two years. He continued making his mark in politics, but at the same time, his interest in business remained high. Joseph was one of several Black businessmen who pooled their resources to start a railroad in early 1870. Named the Enterprise Railroad Company, it carried freight[39] between the Charleston wharves and the railroad depot[40]. Although the group sold the railroad company in 1873, to this day, it remains the only Black-owned railway ever in operation. Under new ownership, the railway went out of business in the 1880s.

DISCUSSION NOTES:

35 – A resolution is an idea or suggestion introduced for others to debate and hopefully pass into law.

36 – A parcel is an area of land; it can be small, like a yard or large, like a farm.

37 – Reconstruction is the time in American history right after the Civil War when Black representatives were an important part of shaping our country for the first time.

38 – Ratified means it was made law.

39 – Freight is a shipment of items which does not contain people or living animals.

40 – The depot is a station, and wharves are at the dock. This is where things are loaded or unloaded. In some instances, people may get on or off here.

HISTORY IS MADE!

In 1870, the United States House of Representatives refused to accept the credentials of a candidate from South Carolina. At the urging of his peers, Joseph Rainey resigned as State Senator to fill that vacant seat. Congress approved him and history was made!

He became the first Black man to be seated as a Congressman. He was sworn in on December 12th, 1870. There were 233 Congressmen, and he was the only Black representative there.

Think how he must have felt! Was he nervous? Maybe. But he was prepared, having learned to read and write, to deliver speeches and mingle with all types of people. He was confident and ready to do what his constituents expected him to do!

The House of Representatives as it appeared in 1857. Congressman Rainey sat in seat #96 on the right-hand side of the House in an aisle seat.

Although his first term was not as an *elected* Congressman, Joseph used that term to learn all about the bills being voted on, formed working partnerships with his House colleagues and knew where and how he would use his position to effect change. Joseph was elected four more times to the House of Representatives. Over time, he was joined by other Black representatives in both Houses. But none of them served as long as he did.

The First Black Members of the U.S. Congress

He served in the Forty-First, Forty-Second, Forty-Third, Forty-Fourth and Forty-Fifth Congresses. This period of American history is called Reconstruction.

During his five terms, he made even more history by becoming the first Black person to preside over the House of Representatives when the Speaker was absent. He was the only Black representative to deliver a eulogy at the funeral of esteemed State Senator Charles Sumner, who had become an ally and a friend in the push for equality for all citizens. Congressman Rainey conducted the *first known sit-in* for equal rights to make people see how unfair things were. He often put himself in danger to show that society was treating its citizens of color unfairly.

The story of the sit-in is one I had heard on my aunt's knee, telling how Congressman Rainey went into a segregated dining room in a Suffolk, Virginia hotel, sat down and asked to be served. When they would not, he refused to leave without being served. After some time, he was picked up and physically thrown out of the front door of the hotel. On that day it had been raining, and he landed face-down in the mud at the bottom of the stairs.

Another incident Aunt Olive told me about was the time he got onto a train. The cars were segregated, meaning that Blacks and whites could not sit in the same railway cars. As the train left the station, Joseph went into the 'whites only' car and took a seat. His appearance would have taken anyone a few moments to see he was a POC. He was a person of upscale bearing, had a light complexion, black silky hair and always dressed exquisitely. The conductor inspected him closely, then told him to go to the 'colored car.' He refused. So, a short while later, after an argument where Joseph refused to move, the conductor told the engineer to stop the train in the middle of nowhere, and they put Joseph off.

Congressman Rainey used his position to call attention to social injustice. He was a strong voice for Native Americans, Chinese immigrant workers and newly freed slaves. He often spoke about these issues with passion and persuasion, gaining the respect of his fellow Congress members, both Black and white. In order for him to be more effective in these areas, they appointed him to the Indian Affairs Bureau and the Freedmen's Committee.

While Reconstruction was a time of great progress and excitement for most, it was also a time of great anger and resentment for some. Many whites, who had been former Confederates or sympathizers, threatened the lives of the Black Republicans and their white allies. Congressman Rainey received many death threats, and the letters were written in bright red ink, symbolizing blood! The promises of violence were often carried out. One representative working to improve the quality of Life for the Freedman was shot and killed as he waited on a railway platform. Although there were witnesses, no one was ever arrested. So, four months after being sworn in, Congressman Rainey, along with Senator Charles Sumner and Prof. John Langston joined together to craft the KKK Act, also known as the Enforcement Act. Senator Sumner was a white Republican from Massachusetts seated in January 1870 who was a firm believer in equality. Professor Langston created the Howard University Law Department in 1869. The three of them felt it was necessary to make a law to protect the Freedmen and their allies.

Some former Confederates had banded together to create a group called The Red Shirts, and they were always looking for ways to keep the Freedmen "in their place"[41]. As they became more popular, they eventually changed their name from The Red Shirts to the KKK or Ku Klux Klan.

He pressed for the passage of the Civil Rights Act of 1871, the Ku Klux Klan Act of 1872 and the Civil Rights Act of 1875. All three were signed into law by President Grant. One of the sections made it a Federal crime to *"molest, interrupt, hinder, or impede the discharge of official duties."* [42] This is one of the laws which was used to prosecute the January 6th Insurrectionists.

These new addendums[43] to the 14th Amendment gave more protection to the Black representatives, Freedmen and their allies. They allowed the President to deploy Federal troops to counter the KKK. And it was necessary due to the constant threats of violence. He had received many letters from his enemies, the last one telling him he should *"prepare to meet your God!"*

They never knew when they would be attacked!

In one instance in 1874, Congressman Rainey was traveling to a scheduled meeting after an inspiring speech in Congress on behalf of one of the Civil Rights Bills. The Red Shirts were determined to be rid of this troublemaker! They knew about the meeting and the route he would take. They decided to get a group together to ambush him. However, Congressman Rainey had been warned, and a large number of supporters were with him. They were joined by U.S. soldiers, all ready to fight his attackers. The would-be assassins, seeing the protection around him, left without a fight and fled into the night.

His enemies were most angry about his continuous crusading[44] on behalf of the Freedmen, the Native Americans and the Chinese railway workers. As a person who had been discriminated[45] against many times, he understood how these groups were being held back from enjoying the full privileges afforded to others. Because he was recognized as a champion of these groups, he also spoke out about the mistreatment of the Chinese railway workers who labored in horrible conditions for pitiful wages with no recourse against their employers.

In spite of the personal verbal and planned physical attacks, Congressman Rainey never let it stop him from doing what the voters had elected him to do and what his conscience demanded.

However, he was concerned for his wife and three children. In 1874, he relocated them to another home in Windsor, Connecticut. But he continued living in Washington DC and kept his residence in Georgetown which was the home he inherited from his father Edward.

This is the home in Windsor, Ct. into which Joseph moved his wife and three children for their protection after he received so many death threats in South Carolina. While he was in Congress, he continued to live in S.C. when the Chamber was in session. (This photo taken in 2000).

The very people who were attacking him the loudest were some of the people he was trying to help. He felt that the best way to heal the division in the country caused by the Civil War was not to punish the South, but to help them regain their dignity and welcome them back into the Union.

He said, *"Our State Convention, which met in 1868, and in which Negroes were a large majority, did not pass any proscriptive or disenfranchising acts, but adopted a liberal constitution, securing alike equal rights to all citizens, White and Black, male and female, as far as possible."*

After he left Congress on March 3rd, 1879, he was appointed a Special Agent for the Treasury Department of South Carolina from May 22nd, 1879 until July 15th, 1881.

Then, he became involved in banking and was a stockholder in various businesses.

DISCUSSION NOTES:

41 – "In their place" was a saying meaning to keep Blacks subservient to whites. They should never feel equal nor expect to be treated as equals.

42 – This is the same law which is being used to prosecute the rioters who broke into the U.S. Capitol Building in Washington, D.C., on January 6, 2021.

43 – Addendum is an addition to a previous law or document. It usually clarifies or adds an issue which was left out.

44 – Crusading is when someone continues to work for a particular cause or group of people.

45 – Discriminated against is when only some people are denied rights, privileges or services, usually because of race or class.

***

Joseph Hayne Rainey died in Georgetown on August 2nd, 1887.

The man is gone. But his legacy lives on! And it was finally acknowledged **126 years** after he last served in Congress. On September 21st, 2005, his official portrait was hung In the Rayburn Building in Washington, DC, giving him the same honor as every other Congressman who has ever been elected.

The portrait which hangs in the Rayburn Building.

"THE LEGACY POEM"

When anyone tells you that you cannot,

Think about this man who said, "*Yes, I can*".

Believe in yourself and prepare for the day

When the right opportunity will come your way.

Never give up and never give in,

If you stop before time, there's no way you'll win.

We each have talents we need to explore,

Don't settle for less when you can do more.

That is the lesson which he's left to us,

It might not be easy, but do it, we must!

Lorna A. Rainey

FAMOUS QUOTATIONS BY CONGRESSMAN RAINEY

"I stand upon the broad plane of right."

"I am contented to be who I am, so long as I have my rights."

"Tell me nothing of a Constitution which fails to shelter beneath its rightful power the people of a Nation."

"We are in earnest for our rights."

FIRST IN THE HOUSE – PHOTO GALLERY

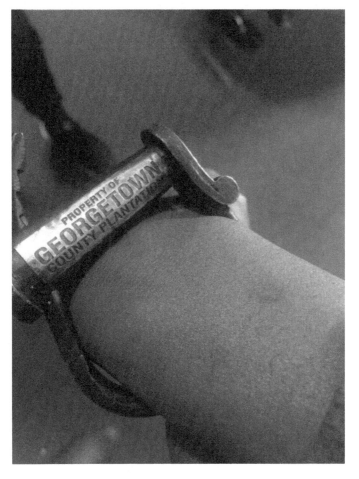

Slave shackles locked onto the wrist or ankles. Not only does it make escape impossible, but it also clearly identifies the plantation to which the enslaved person belongs, so if they are caught, they can be returned to their owner.

Olive Rainey with the desk her father Joseph Rainey used in his Congressional office.

I SAY TO YOU GENTLEMEN, THAT THIS
DISCRIMINATION AGAINST THE NEGRO RACE
IN THIS COUNTRY IS UNJUST, IS UNWORTHY
OF A HIGH-MINDED PEOPLE WHOSE EXAMPLE
SHOULD HAVE A SALUTARY INFLUENCE IN THE
WORLD.

- JOSEPH HAYNE RAINEY -

JOSEPH RAINEY – Letter to Sen. Sumner

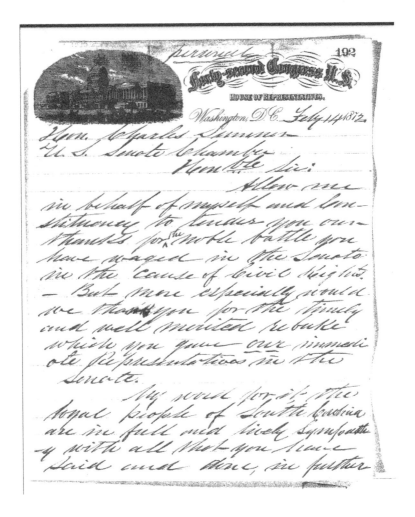

ance of this essential and
highly important measure—
despite windy and flimsy declarations to the contrary.

Believe me Sir, if the
prayer of the oppressed prevails
you will live long in po-
litical & social prosperity
when your enemies will
have been forgotten.

- Our prayer is that
a halo of glory may ever-
rest upon your princely
brow—

With high esteem,
I have the honor to re-
main yours gratefully,
[signature]

Transcription Of The Letter:

July 14, 1872
Hon. Charles Sumner
U.S. Senate Chamber

 Humble Sir:

Allow me in behalf of myself and constituency to tender you our thanks for the noble battle you have waged in the Senate in the cause of Civil Rights.

But more especially would we thank you for the timely and well merited rebuke which you gave our immediate Representatives in the Senate.

My word for it, the loyal people of South Carolina are in full and lively sympathy with all that you have said and done in furtherance of the essential and mighty important measure despite windy and spleeny declarations to the contrary.

Believe me Sir, if the prayer of the oppressed prevails you will live long in political and social prosperity when your enemies will have been forgotten.

 Our prayer is that a halo of glory may ever rest upon your princely brow.

With high esteem, I have the honor to remain yours gratefully,

 J.H. Rainey

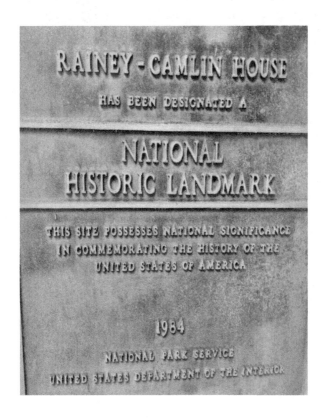

*The marker on the fence post outside Rainey-
Camlin House in Georgetown, S.C.*

Four pieces of the Rainey silverware. The fork and knife are engraved with "R". The serving spoon with "JHR" engraved, and the baby spoon belonging to Olive Rainey is engraved with "OAR".

The Joseph Rainey exhibit at the new International
African American Museum in Charleston, S.C.

Joseph Rainey Park at night. Located in Georgetown, S.C.

Dedication of Joseph H. Rainey Room in the Capitol Building, Washington, DC

February 9th, 2022

Pictured from left to right: Cong. Joyce Beatty (Oh), Cong. Tom Rice (S.C.), Lorna A. Rainey, Cong. Steve Scalise (La), Cong. James Clyburn (S.C.), Cong. Nancy Pelosi (House Speaker- Ca), Nashota Rainey-Webb, Datu Faison, Meredith Rainey-Valmon & Ellyn-Hazel Rainey.

The Plaque at the Joseph H. Rainey Room

This plaque, dedicated on February 9th, 2022, is outside the entrance to Room H-150, the same room in which Congressman Rainey often worked when he was in office.

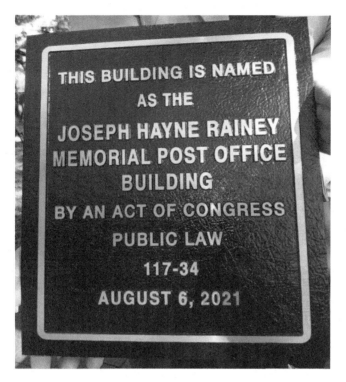

Congressman Tim Rice (S.C) brought a motion onto the Congressional floor to propose that the new Main Post Office in Georgetown, S.C., be named after Congressman Rainey. This can only be done with the consent of Congress and the Postmaster General. The motion was approved, and on November 9th, 2021, we had the official plaque presentation. When the P.O. was completed, this plaque was mounted in the lobby.

The exterior of the beautiful new United States Post Office. This is a great honor since they normally do not name P.O. buildings after people. They are usually named for their location. Think about it. What is the name of the Post Office where you live?

ACKNOWLEDGEMENTS

Although most of the information in this book is readily available through many diverse sources, I acknowledge the following due to their exceptional contribution to the furtherance of disseminating information about Congressman Rainey:

Bermuda Gazette (now The Royal Gazette)

Bermuda National Trust – Anna Stevenson (*Heritage Education Coordinator)*, Dr. Charlotte Andrews *(Head of Cultural Heritage), Chris Davis (Museums Manager)*

Congressman James Clyburn (S.C.)

Cong. Gregory Meeks (N.Y.)

Congressman Steve Scalise (La.)

Congressman Tim Rice (S.C.)

Dr. Bobby Donaldson – Assoc. Professor of History & Director/Center for Civil Rights History and Research (U. of S.C.)

Dr. Felice Knight - International African-American Museum

Dr. Tonya Matthews – Director of Education / International African American Museum

Elizabeth Ratigan – Kiplinger Research Library

Emerald Garrett – Sr. Legislative Assistant/Cong. James Clyburn

Gullah Museum – Georgetown, S.C.

Hon. Carol Jayroe – Mayor of Georgetown, S.C.

History, Art & Archives – U.S. House of Representatives

Karol Anderson – Chairman Georgetown County Republican Party

Mr. Christopher Frear – Lead writer and Researcher/Center for Civil Rights History and Research (U. of S.C.)

Mr. Dean Love – Producer-Director / Dean Love Films

Mr. James Fitch – Owner/Rice Museum in Georgetown, S.C.

Mr. Marvin Neal – President NAACP Georgetown Branch

Mr. Ronn Jackson – U.S. Capitol Visitor Services Division

Mr. Wayne Wood – Sports icon and investment counselor

Richard Camlin – Owner of Rainey-Camlin House in Georgetown, S.C.

Steve Williams – Author / "24 Extraordinary People Who Made A Difference"

Tina Stevenson – Publisher and Editor in Chief / "The Bermudian"

World Community Magazine – Edward McQueen Joelle McQueen, and April Gardner

"House Beautiful: Colonial Homes" – February 1996

Smithsonian Magazine

South Carolina Department of Education

Cyril O. Packwood (author) – "Detour-Bermuda:
Destination-U.S. House of Representatives"

Former House Speaker Madame Cong. Nancy Pelosi

Robyn Rainey-Wingate

Made in United States
North Haven, CT
15 June 2025

69833405R00046